HIDE AND SEEK

Animals

DK

A Dorling Kindersley Book

Notes for parents

Hide and Seek Animals is a wonderful picture book for you and your child to share. From pets and farm animals to wildlife and dinosaurs, every page is filled with creatures to find and talk about. Amazing photographs and bright, make-believe scenes show animals from around the globe, and will help your child to develop observation skills, build vocabulary, learn colours, and practise counting.

To get the most out of this book

- Talk about the animals you can see on each page. Point to them, say their names, then hunt for each one together. As children become familiar with the book, they will be able to name and find the animals themselves.
- Encourage your child to describe the different creatures. What colour are they? Are they furry, feathery, wrinkly, scaly, patterned, or plain? What noises do they make? Where do they live and how do they move? Which one is your child's favourite?
- Read the rhymes and let your child say them with you. Then help your child find the animals and objects in the rhymes.
- Once your child knows letter sounds, you can play traditional "I Spy". Ask your child to spot an animal that begins with a certain letter.

Written by Sarah Davis and Dawn Sirett
Edited by Charlie Gardner and Phil Hunt
Designed by Rachael Parfitt Hunt and Victoria Palastanga
Illustrations by Angela Muss and Paul Nicholls
Additional illustrations Rachael Parfitt Hunt and Dave Ball
Production Controller Jen Lockwood
Production Editor Siu Yin Chan

First published in Great Britain in 2011 by Dorling Kindersley Limited, 80 Strand, London WC2R 0RL

Copyright © 2011 Dorling Kindersley Limited

LONDON, NEW YORK, MELBOURNE, MUNICH, AND DELHI

A Penguin Company
4 6 8 10 9 7 5
013–179426–June/2011

A CIP catalogue record for this book is available from the British Library.

ISBN: 978-1-40536-389-1

All rights reserved. No part of this publication may be reproduced, stored in a retrieval system, or transmitted in any form or by any means, electronic, mechanical, photocopying, recording, or otherwise, without the prior written permission of the copyright owner.

Printed and bound in China by Leo Paper Products

Discover more at **www.dk.com**

Picture Credits

The publisher would like to thank the following for their kind permission to reproduce their photographs:
(Key: a-above; b-below/bottom; c-centre; f-far; l-left; r-right; t-top)

Alamy Images: Arco Images GmbH / I. Schulz 36crb, 37cr, 37bc; Brand X Pictures 42crb/8 (bug), 43fcr (bug); Erik Lam 6c (jack russell); Life on white 2bc, 26fbr, 27ftr, 44ca, 44fcrb; Kevin Schafer 27crb, 42br/8 (bird), 43ftr (macaw); Peter Titmuss 8bc (horse), 9cl; Top-Pics TBK 30cb (seal), 31c (seal); WildLife GmbH 30cr (reindeer), 30bl (reindeer), 44fcla (reindeer), 45tc. **Corbis:** Hal Beral 1cra (grouper fish), 1br (grouper fish), 20cb (grouper fish), 21tl (grouper fish x2), 21clb (grouper fish), 42br/9 (fish), 43cla (red fish), 44tl (fish), 44fcr; David Campbell / Visuals Unlimited 28ftr, 29crb; DLILLC 26clb, 27cra (frog), 44tc (frog), 44br; Martin Harvey 20fcr (striped fish x5), 21fcla (striped fish x10), 21fcl (striped fish x4), 21fbr (striped fish), 42bl/2 (fish), 43fcra (striped fish); Steven Kazlowski / Science Faction 30tl (walrus), 31cb (walrus); Frans Lanting 20cl, 47clb; Robert Llewellyn 20tr (starfish x5), 20bl (starfish), 20br (starfish), 20fbl (starfish), 21fbl (starfish), 21fbr (starfish); Steve Maslowski / Visuals Unlimited 28fcr (shrew); Don Mason 8crb (dog), 8fclb (dog); Arthur Morris 1fcra (warbler), 1fclb (warbler); Ocean 10tr, 11br (cow); Winfried Wisniewski / Zefa 20fbr (crab), 21tc (crab x2), 21fbl (crab); Norbert Wu / Science Faction 1clb (jellyfish), 1ftl (jellyfish), 21ca (jellyfish x4), 21cl (jellyfish x4). **Dorling Kindersley:** Booth Museum of Natural History, Brighton 42cla/1 (butterfly), 43cb (butterfly); Robert L. Braun - modelmaker 3fbl, 34bl (stegosaurus), 34-35 (stegosaurus); Centaur Studios - modelmakers 34tc (triceratops), 35bc; Philip Dowell 26fcla, 27cla, 27fcrb (leopard), 33fcrb (goat), 47fcra; Graham High at Centaur Studios - modelmaker 34c (brachiosaurus), 34br, 35cl (brachiosaurus); Jon Hughes 34cl (heterodontosaurus), 35c (heterodontosaurus); Hunstanton Sea Life Centre, Hunstanton, Norfolk 36cl, 37cl, 37bl; Jeremy Hunt - modelmaker 20cr (shark); Natural History Museum, London 1tl (butterfly), 1tr (assassin bug), 1cla (assassin bug), 1clb (butterfly), 1crb (assassin bug), 1bl (assassin bug), 1ftr (butterfly x2), 1fcrb (butterfly), 2cra, 12tc, 12cra (butterfly x3), 12fcra (bug), 12fcl (moth), 13tc (moth), 13c (millipede), 13c (red bug), 13ftl (butterfly), 13fcr (butterfly), 13fclb (beetle), 13fbl (butterfly), 20bc (shell x2), 21br (shell), 21fbl (shell), 26fcra, 27cra (bug), 27cr, 27cr (bug), 27fcla, 27fcrb (bug x3), 34bc (gallimimus), 34cra (oviraptor), 34cl (deinonychus), 35fcl, 35fcra (gallimimus), 39cla (butterfly), 39cl (butterfly), 39cr (butterfly), 39bc (butterfly), 39br (butterfly), 39fcra (butterfly), 42cla/3 (butterfly), 42clb/2 (bug), 42cb/5 (bug), 42fclb/1 (bug), 43tl (butterfly), 43ca (bug), 43crb (bug), 43fbl (bug), 44c, 45cra; Stephen Oliver 33clb (chick); David Peart 1ca (turtle), 1crb (turtle), 1bc (turtle), 20ca (turtle x4); Luis V. Rey 34cr (velociraptor), 34clb (velociraptor); Royal Tyrrell Museum of Palaeontology, Alberta, Canada 34cla (troodon), 34fcr, 34tl (edmontonia), 34-35 (edmontonia); South of England Rare Breeds Centre, Ashford, Kent 10tl/1 (goose), 10clb (goose), 10crb (ducks); Barrie Watts 1cla (duckling), 1bl (duckling); Weymouth Sea Life Centre 1cla (octopus), 1bl (octopus), 1fcra (octopus), 1fbr (octopus), 2tr (octopus), 20c (octopus), 21cla; Jerry Young 24br (crocodile), 27cl, 42cb/4 (bug), 43fcrb (red bug). **FLPA:** Jim Brandenburg / Minden Pictures 28c, 29tl; Flip De Nooyer / FN / Minden 22cl (otter), 22fcl (cormorant), 23tr (cormorant), 23ftr (otter); Gerry Ellis / Minden Pictures 25crb (bird), 25bl, 46bl, 46bc (bird); Michael & Patricia Fogden / Minden Pictures 18fcrb, 45ca; Sebastian Kennerknecht / Minden Pictures 19bc; Heidi & Hans-Juergen Koch / Minden Pictures 19ca; Pete Oxford / Minden Pictures 38fbr, 39tl; Cyril Ruoso / Minden Pictures 19fcrb; Tom Vezo / Minden Pictures 18c (gila), 18fbr, 28cra (ground squirrel), 28cr (ground squirrel); Norbert Wu / Minden Pictures 30cl (icefish), 31c (icefish). **Fotolia:** Steve Byland 14bl (swan x3), 14tr (swan x 2), 15ftl (swan); Eric Isselée 1fbr (dog), 6cr (border collie), 7fbr (bull terrier), 14tc (vulture), 15tl (vulture); Michael Pettigrew 7c. **Getty Images:** Botanica / Picavet 22cr (eel), 22ftl/1 (eel x3), 23clb (eel x2); Brand X Pictures 12fcrb/1 (firefly x6), 13tr (firefly), 13c (firefly), 13clb (firefly), 13ftl (firefly), 13fcra (firefly), 13fcrb (firefly), 13fbr (firefly); Comstock Images 24ftl/3 (giraffe), 24ftr, 24fcl, 25fcr/2 (giraffe); Digital Vision / Digital Zoo 32cl, 33cl; Digital Vision / Martin Harvey 25c/2 (lion cub); Discovery Channel Images / Jeff Foott 24tr (ants x3), 24bl (ants), 24br (ants); First Light / Doug Hamilton 22tc (duck x3), 23tc (duck), 23cla (duck), 23ca (duck), 42br/7 (bird), 43fcla (duck); First Light / Ken Gillespie 16cra, 17crb; First Light / Thomas Kitchin & Victoria Hurst 22fcl (salmon x4), 22fcrb, 23clb (salmon), 23crb, 23fcl; Flickr / Bill Wakeley Photography 16cl, 16cr (bird), 17cra (cardinal x3), 17fcr (cardinal); Flickr / Bucks Wildlife Photography 16fcla/2 (eagle), 17fcr (eagle); Flickr / Eddie Sin 25fbl; Flickr / Gail Shotlander 25ftl, 25fcl; Flickr / Paul Lee 25cr/2 (wildebeest); Flickr / Rick Poon 19fbr; Gallo Images / Daryl Balfour 25crb (squirrel); Gallo Images / George Brits 24fcr (jackal), 25cra; Gallo Images / Heinrich van den Berg 18ca, 19fcra, 23c (moorhen); Gallo Images / Roger de la Harpe 18clb, 19cl; Gallo Images / Shem Compion 24fbr (beetle), 47cb; Martin Harvey / Lifesize 3fclb (lion cub), 25cl/1 (lion cub); Koki Iino 9cr (mouse); Image Source 25tl, 25fcrb, 25fbr; The Image Bank / Darrin Klimek 18cr, 18fbl (snake); The Image Bank / Joseph Devenney 18cra, 18bl; The Image Bank / Winfried Wisniewski 16fcl, 17fcla (goshawk); Lifesize / Don Farrall 22clb (frog x2), 23cra (frog), 23fcr (frog); National Geographic / George Grall 29ca, 29cb; National Geographic / Gordon Wiltsie 26crb, 27fbr; National Geographic / Joel Sartore 17fcl, 18cl (glass lizard), 19fbl, 28ca (badger), 29c, 42cl (armadillo x4), 43ca (armadillo), 43cra (armadillo), 43cb (armadillo), 43br (armadillo); Panoramic Images 24fcr (bird), 25tc (bird x2), 25fcr (bird), 32fcr, 33crb (lion); Photodisc / Digital Zoo 29cr (skunk), 29ftl; Photodisc / Life On White 16bl, 17ftl (skunk), 28ca (prairie dog), 28clb, 28fcra (chipmunk), 29cl; Photodisc / Martin Harvey 16ftr, 17fcrb (raccoon); Photodisc / Paul E. Tessier 24fcl (bird), 28fcr (owl), 29tc; Photodisc / Steve Allen 24crb; Photodisc / Sylvain Cordier 16fcla/1 (eagle), 17c (eagle); Photodisc / Theo Allofs 25cb (ostrich), 46fbr; Photographer's Choice / Annie Katz 24cb (hippo); Photographer's Choice / Burazin 24cl (giraffe), 24ftl/1 (giraffe), 24ftl/2 (giraffe), 25fcr/1 (giraffe); Photographer's Choice / Cristian Baitg 18c (chameleon), 19c; Photographer's Choice / Darrell Gulin 1tc (butterfly), 1cla (butterfly), 1ca (butterfly), 1cb (butterfly), 1bl (butterfly), 1bc (butterfly), 26tc (butterfly x4), 27tc (butterfly x2), 27cb, 27fcr, 28cr (butterfly), 29cr (butterfly), 38clb, 39cb, 48tl; Photographer's Choice / Frank Lukasseck 30bc (wolf), 31fcrb, 32tc, 33cr (penguins); Photographer's Choice / Martin Harvey 25crb (vulture); Photographer's Choice / Pam Francis 32bc (pig x3), 33tr (pig), 33fcl (pig), 33fbl (pig); Photolibrary / Robin Redfern 22fclb (vole), 23fcr (vole); Photolibrary / Stan Osolinski 18tl, 19cr; Photonica / Tariq Dajani 16crb, 17fcra; Photonica / Zac Macaulay 19cra (turtle); Riser / GK Hart / Vikki Hart 22tc/4 (ducks), 22fcra; Riser / JH Pete Carmichael 18ftr, 19fcl; Riser / Kevin Schafer 19fclb; Riser / Richard Drury 28tr, 28cl; Robert Harding World Imagery / James Hager 18crb, 18ftl; Science Faction / Chip Simons 18br, 18fbl; Stock Image / Frank Lukasseck 22ftr, 42bc/4 (bird), 43tc (egret); Stockbyte / Altrendo Nature 25cl (vulture); Stockbyte / John Foxx 24fbl; Stockbyte / Tom Brakefield 24bl (spider), 24bc (spider), 24fbr (spider); Stone / Art Wolfe 2ftl (elephant), 24cla (elephant), 25bc (elephant); Stone / Catherine Ledner 28bc, 29fcla; Stone / Gravity Giant Productions 25cla (baboon), 25br; Stone / Jonathan Knowles 24cb (porcupine x2); Stone / Paul Taylor 22tr, 22fcla (damselfly x2), 23ftr (damselfly); Stone+ / Catherine Ledner 16tr, 17fbr; Taxi / Giel 16cb, 17tl (bear); Wim van den Heever 25c/1 (wildebeest); Visuals Unlimited / Joe McDonald 18fcra, 29cla, 29br; Workbook Stock / David Maitland 19cb, 47cr; Workbook Stock / Thomas Kokta 32clb, 33tc (seal); Workbook Stock / Tier Und Naturfotografie J & C Sohns 16fclb (porcupine), 17tc (porcupine). **imagequestmarine.com:** 20cb (sea krait), 20ftr (sea krait x2), 21crb (sea krait). **iStockphoto.com:** Robert Blanchard 14clb (spoonbill), 15cra (spoonbill), 42bc/5 (bird), 43cr (spoonbill); Sascha Burkard 1cla (tree frog), 1cb (tree frog), 1bl (tree frog), 1fcra (tree frog), 1fcrb (tree frog), 1fbl (tree frog); Nicola Destefano 14cb (turtledove), 15fclb (turtledove); Shunyu Fan 1ca (nest), 1bc (nest), 15clb (nest); Mehmet Salih Guler 6cl (doberman); Bjorn Heller 10c (tractor), 47br; Andrew Howe 1tc (swift), 1cra (robin), 1cb (swift), 1ftl (swift), 1fcla (swift), 1fclb (swift), 14tr (swift), 14cla (blackbird), 14c (magpie x2), 14bc (kingfisher), 14fcra (swallow), 14fclb (swallow), 15tc (swift), 15cla (robin), 15cla (tit), 15c (kingfisher), 15c (magpie), 15clb (blackbird), 15cb (tit), 15fcla (magpie), 15fcra (swift), 15fcl (robin), 15fcl (tit), 15fcl (wren), 42bl/1 (bird), 42bl/3 (bird), 42br/9 (bird), 43clb (swallow), 43cb (kingfisher), 43br (robin); Eric Isselée 1clb (panda), 3cr, 6fbl (jack russell), 38fbl, 39tr, 42tl (panda), 42clb/3 (dog), 43c, 43bc (dog); Karel Broz 14ftl/1 (macaw x2), 14fcr, 15fcla (macaw); Martin Kraft 1fcla (giraffe), 1fbl (giraffe); Cay-Uwe Kulzer 14fcla (woodpecker), 15c (woodpecker); Adam Mattel 1tl (snake), 1tr (snake), 1cb (snake), 1crb (snake), 1ftr (snake), 1fcrb (snake); Christian Musat 3fcla, 24cra/1 (zebra), 24c (zebra), 38cla, 39bl; Skip ODonnell 38fcr, 39bc; Thomas Sztanek 14fcl (lorikeet), 15fcr (lorikeet); Paul Tessier 14tl (puffin), 14ca (mallard), 14cl (hummingbird), 14cr, 15bc, 15fbr (mallard), 42bc/6 (bird), 43fcr (hummingbird). **Lonely Planet Images:** Holger Leue 16ca (bear), 17bl. **naturepl.com:** Doug Allan 30fbl (narwhal), 31ftl (narwhal); Eric Baccega 31fcl; John Cancalosi 30tr; Robin Chittenden 30cb (goose), 30fcra; Brandon Cole 30c (beluga whale), 31bc; Elio Della Ferrera 30cla (ermine), 31cla; Steven Kazlowski 30ca/1 (arctic fox), 30ca/2 (arctic fox), 30c (seal), 30cr (fox), 30ftr, 30fcl (polar bear), 31ca, 31fcra (seal), 31fbl, 47crb, 47fcrb; Bengt Lundberg 30cb (lemming), 31crb; Juan Carlos Munoz 30fcl (wolverine), 30fbr; Doug Perrine 30tc (shark), 30br; Gabriel Rojo 31fcr; Andy Rouse 30clb (owl), 31tc; Shattil & Rozinski 1crb (jay), 36ca, 37cb, 37fbl, 42bl/2 (bird), 43tr (jay); Gary K. Smith 30fclb (seal), 30fcrb; Tom Vezo 31br; Wild Wonders of Europe / Zacek 30fcla (owl), 31fclb. **Photolibrary:** Martyn Chillmaid / Oxford Scientific (OSF) 17ca (snake), 17c (snake); Mark Deeble & Victoria Stone 24cr (bat eared fox), 25ca (bat eared fox); Juniors Bildarchiv 1cla (killer whale), 1bl (killer whale), 3ftr, 20tr (killer whale), 21cr (killer whale), 38tc, 39cla; Oxford Scientific (OSF) / Ariadne Van Zandbergen 1ca (chameleon), 1cb (chameleon), 1bc (chameleon), 1fclb (chameleon), 26fbl, 27fclb. **Science Photo Library:** Barbara Strnadova 42cla/2 (butterfly), 43crb (butterfly). **SeaPics.com:** 20ftr (sunfish), 21c (sunfish). **Warren Photographic:** 1clb (lemur), 1fcra (kitten), 1fbr (kitten), 2cla, 8tl (rabbits), 8tc (dog), 8tr, 8ca/1 (goldfish), 8ca/2 (goldfish), 8cra, 8cl (cats), 8bl (budgerigars), 8ftl (parrots), 8ftr, 8fcl (tortoise), 8fcl (stick insect x2), 8fcr, 9cra, 9cr (chinchilla), 9bc (stick insect x2), 9br, 9ftl, 9fcla, 9fcr, 9fcrb (cats), 9fbr, 10bc (ducklings), 11clb (goat), 24cl (springbok), 25fcla, 28fcla, 29bc, 32cr/1 (rabbit x6), 32cb, 32crb/1 (cat), 32crb/2 (cat), 32fcra (mallard duckling), 33tl (rabbit), 33tr (rabbit), 33cra (rabbit), 33bc (cat), 33ftl (duck), 33ftr (cat), 33fcla (rabbit), 33fcr (rabbit), 33fclb (lamb), 33fbr (rabbit), 36cra, 37tl, 37br, 38bc, 39cl, 42cl/4 (rabbit), 42bc/7 (fish), 43tr (goldfish), 43cra (sandy rabbit); Jane Burton 1tc (dog), 1cb (dog), 3ftl, 3fcr (cat), 4cb, 4bl, 4ftl, 4fcl, 5tl, 5c, 5cr, 5ftl, 6tc (pomeranian), 6tc (schnauzer), 6tr (pugzu), 6cr (pugzu), 6cb (boxer), 6crb (shih tzu), 6bl, 6ftl, 6fcra (spaniel), 6fcr, 6fclb (shih tzu), 6fbr, 7ca (shih tzu x2), 7cra (chihuahua x2), 7clb (chihuahua), 7clb (spaniel), 7crb (bulldog pup x2), 7crb (bulldog), 7bl (schnauzer), 7bc (pomeranian), 7ftl/1 (dachshunds x2), 7fcla (bulldog pup x2), 7fcla (bulldog), 7fbr (dachshund), 11c, 16ca/1 (fox), 16ca/2 (fox), 16c (fox), 16clb (rabbit x2), 16fcr, 16fbr (rabbit x2), 17ca (rabbit x6), 17br, 17fcrb (rabbit), 28cr (rabbit), 28br, 28fbr, 29tr (rabbit x4), 29fcl, 32cla, 33fcr (dog), 42cl/3 (cat), 42c/4 (cat), 42c/5 (rabbit), 42clb/2 (dog), 42cb/5 (dog), 42crb/6 (dog), 42fcl/1 (rabbit), 42fclb/1 (dog), 43cra (grey rabbit), 43cl (shih tzu), 43clb (boxer), 43cb (rabbit), 43bl (cat), 43ftl (bulldog), 43fcrb (cat), 43fbl (dog), 44clb, 44ftl (cat), 45cb, 45bl, 48tr; Kim Taylor 5cra, 16cla (squirrel), 16cr (squirrel), 16fcr (bat), 17cr (bat); Mark Taylor 1ftl (dog), 1fcra (dog), 4fbl, 5fcrb, 6tl, 6crb (yorkie), 6br, 6ftr (poodle), 6fcl (yorkie), 7tc (labrador x2), 7c (beagle), 7cb (labrador), 7fcl (poodle), 16fcra, 17clb, 32fcl, 33tc (fawn), 42cr/6 (cat), 42cb/4 (dog), 42crb/7 (dog), 43cl (poodle), 43br (dog), 43fcl (grey cat).

Jacket images: *Front:* **Alamy Images:** Brand X Pictures tl (green bug); Life on white c (tiger). **Dorling Kindersley:** Natural History Museum, London tl (assassin bug), bl (assassin bug), crb (butterfly); Barrie Watts cla (duckling). **Getty Images:** Photographer's Choice / Darrell Gulin tc (butterfly), cr (butterfly). **iStockphoto.com:** Sascha Burkard bc (tree frog); Eric Isselée cra (dog), fclb (panda); Martin Kraft fcrb (giraffe); Adam Mattel ftr (snake). **Photolibrary:** Oxford Scientific (OSF) / Ariadne Van Zandbergen fbl (chameleon). **Warren Photographic:** ca (rooster). *Back:* **Dorling Kindersley:** Natural History Museum, London ftl (bug); David Peart fcla (turtle). **iStockphoto.com:** Sascha Burkard fcr (tree frog); Eric Isselée fcrb (panda). **Warren Photographic:** fcr (kitten).

All other images © Dorling Kindersley. For further information see: www.dkimages.com

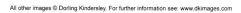

a Bulldog

a zebra

a ladybird

a seahorse

a lion cub

a dinosaur

Contents

a killer whale

a chick

a cat

a donkey

Boo!

This is Hoppity Frog! He's in every scene in this book! See if you can spot him again and again.

Meow!

Let's find...

5 Siamese cats

a cat collar

a silver
spotted cat

4 cat paw prints

a Manx cat
(a cat with no tail)

a brown cat

a toy cat

a black cat

a red tabby cat

a cream cat and
a grey kitten

a black-and-white
cat

a Sphynx cat

3 toy mice

a silver-blue cat

I spy a cat
in front of the moon.
I think
you'll spot him
very soon.

a Birman cat

a Persian cat

a tortoiseshell cat

Woof! Woof!

Let's find...

a Poodle

a German Shepherd

a Beagle

a Pomeranian

a Miniature Schnauzer

a Pug

a Cocker Spaniel

3 Dachshunds

2 Labradors

**Find the doggy bones.
There are three.
Where are they hiding?
Can you see?**

a Bulldog
and 2 puppies

a dog lead

4 food bowls

2 Shih tzu

2 Chihuahuas

a toy dog

My pets

Let's find...

2 parrots

3 rabbits

a dog

a canary

2 guinea pigs

2 goldfish

2 stick insects

a cat and kitten

a terrapin

a tortoise

a gerbil

a puppy

a black horse

2 lovebirds

a cockatoo

a chestnut pony

2 budgies

8

Mirror, mirror
on the wall,
where's the reptile
with no legs
at all?

9

On the farm

Let's find...

a black sheep

2 geese

a black-and-white cow

4 white ducks

a spotty pig

a cockerel

a calf

4 lambs

3 piglets

a billy goat

a sheep dog

a foal

a donkey

a black-and-white bull

I spy a mouse upon the ground. When you see him, make a squeaky sound!

Creepy crawlies!

Let's find...

3 spiders

4 flies

a millipede

a wasp

4 snails

a dragonfly

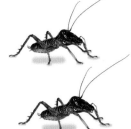

2 crickets

2 bees

3 butterflies

a beetle

a locust

a moth

5 slugs

a thorn bug

2 earthworms

6 fireflies

7 ladybirds

a mite

2 leaf insects

6 woodlice

2 caterpillars

a digger wasp

a spider hunting wasp

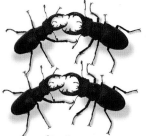

4 stag beetles

Can you find five marching ants? I hope they're not inside your pants!

Tweet!

Let's find...

2 macaws

a puffin

a vulture

a woodpecker

a blackbird

a mallard

a rainbow lorikeet

a hummingbird

2 magpies

a swallow

a spoonbill

a dove

an ostrich

3 swans

a kingfisher

14

Spot the eggs
laid in a nest,
then choose the bird
that you like best.

Wild woods

Let's find...

2 bald eagles

a grey squirrel

a grizzly bear

2 foxes

a white-tailed deer

an American beaver

a racoon

a white-tailed fawn

16

a striped
skunk

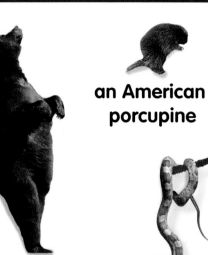

an American
porcupine

a weasel

I see an owl.
Can you see him, too?
When you do,
shout, "Twit-twoo!"

goshawk

a black bear

a rat snake

6 wild rabbits

3 cardinal
birds

a wild boar

Reptiles

Let's find...

2 tortoises

a crocodile

a caiman

a Thai water dragon

a glass lizard

a chameleon

a Gila monster

a western diamondback rattlesnake

a spotty, stripy gecko

a milk snake

a rat snake

a European green lizard

a desert iguana

an alligator

18

Floating
oh so gracefully,
find two turtles
in the sea.

Splish! Splash!

Let's find...

3 hermit crabs

3 seahorses

2 green sea turtles

5 brown starfish

a killer whale

2 banded sea snakes

an ocean sunfish

20

4 angelfish

2 coral groupers

2 ghost crabs

10 longfin bannerfish

a blue-ringed octopus

4 box jellyfish

I spy
a beautiful sight,
four clownfish,
orange and white.

21

Rivers

Let's find...

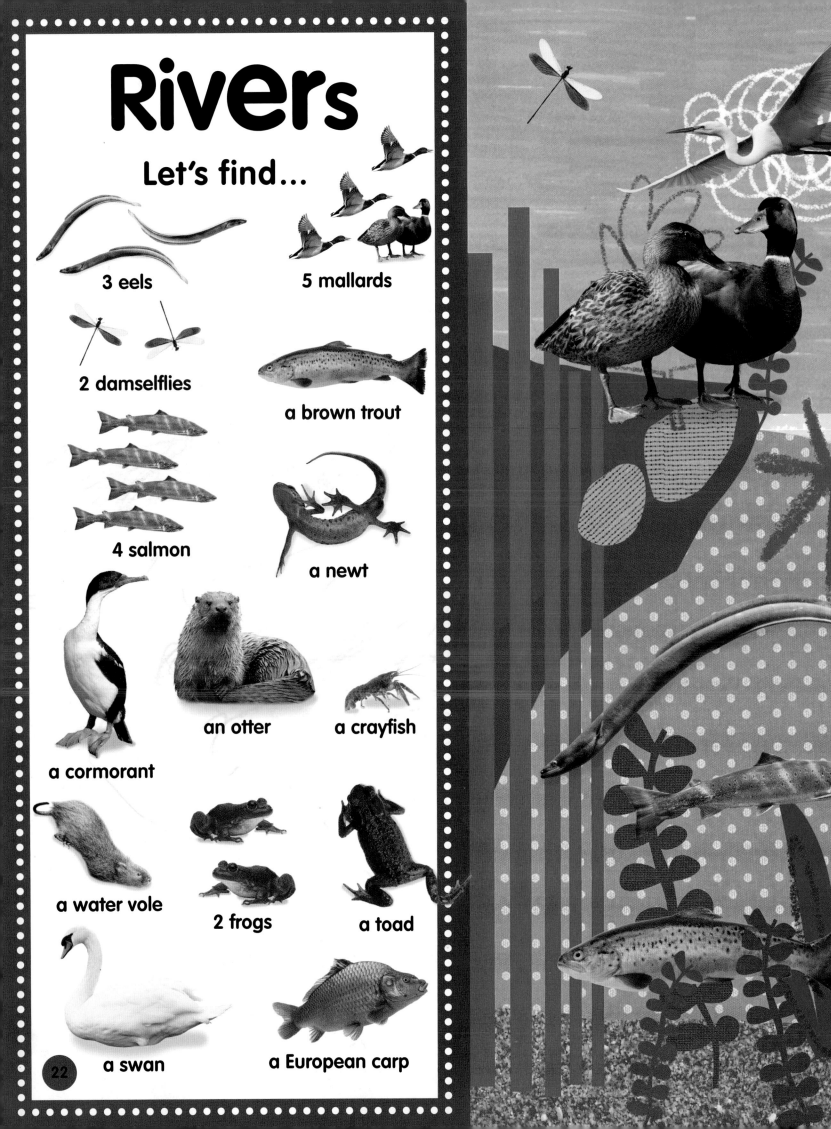

3 eels

5 mallards

2 damselflies

a brown trout

4 salmon

a newt

a cormorant

an otter

a crayfish

a water vole

2 frogs

a toad

a swan

a European carp

Look for three
small blue-eyed fish
called sticklebacks,
splish, splash, splish!

On safari

Let's find...

3 giraffes

an African elephant

2 zebras

6 harvester ants

an African bison

a bushbaby

24

a white
rhinoceros

a warthog

2 secretary
birds

a lion and lioness

a gazelle

a baboon

a cheetah

a bat-eared
fox

a jackal

I spy
two
porcupines.
Watch out
for their
prickly spines!

Jungle

Let's find...

a chimpanzee

4 morpho butterflies

a toucan

a jaguar

a poison dart frog

an orang-utan

5 piranhas

a gorilla

a red-eyed tree frog

a tarantula

an Asian elephant

a chameleon

a jumping spider

a sloth

a tiger

Five stripy beetles, can you find them all?
Look carefully, for they are quite small.

Burrowers

a fox

a pocket mouse

Let's find...

a mole

7 ants

an American badger

a prairie dog

a thirteen-lined ground squirrel

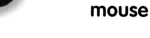
a chipmunk

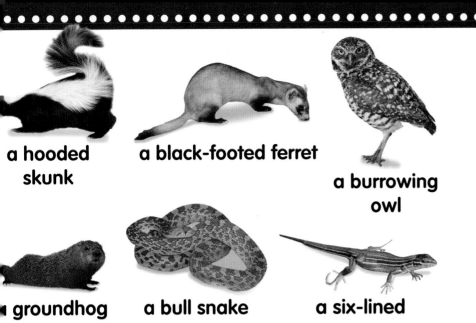

a hooded skunk

a black-footed ferret

a burrowing owl

groundhog

a bull snake

a six-lined race runner

4 rabbits

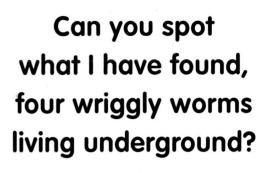

Can you spot what I have found, four wriggly worms living underground?

Snowy animals

Let's find...

an emperor
penguin

a walrus

a Greenland shark

a great
grey owl

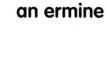
an ermine

2 Arctic foxes

a polar
bear cub

an icefish

a beluga
whale

a bearded seal

a wolverine

a crab-eater
seal

a grey seal
pup

a snowy owl

a lemming

a narwhal

a reindeer

a grey wolf

30

Where's the
Arctic hare?
I think I know.
Her winter fur
is as white as snow.

31

Baby animals

Let's find...

an ostrich chick

a Dachshund puppy

4 penguin chicks

5 ducklings

a fawn

an elephant calf

6 baby rabbits

a lion cub

2 fox cubs

a seal pup

a lamb

4 kittens

2 owl chicks

a pony foal

3 piglets

Are you clever?
Are you quick?
Can you spot
a yellow chick?

Dinosaurs

Let's find...

a Triceratops

a Troodon

an Apatosaurus

a Heterodontosaurus

a Brachiosaurus

a Deinonychus

a Pentaceratops

a Velociraptor

a Saltasaurus

a Stegosaurus

a Gallimimus

I spy a
frightening sight,
a mighty T-rex
about to bite!

Matching

Let's find the other halves of these jigsaw animals.

a seal

a jay

a ring-tailed lemur

a Chinese peacock butterfly

a dolphin

There are five caterpillars
for you to seek.
Count them
as they crawl and creep.

lemur

a ring-tailed

a Chinese peacock
butterfly

a jay   a seal   a dolphin

The answers

37

Animal patterns

Let's find the pattern for...

a tiger

a killer whale

an elephant

a toucan

a zebra

a chick

a cheetah

a butterfly

a frog

a flamingo

a koala

a beetle

a kitten

a ladybird

a snake

There are six stripy moths
I can see.
Where have they landed?
Please show me.

Silhouettes

an aardvark

a bat

Let's find...

a sea lion

a kangaroo

2 houseflies

an ostrich

3 centipedes

a puffin

40

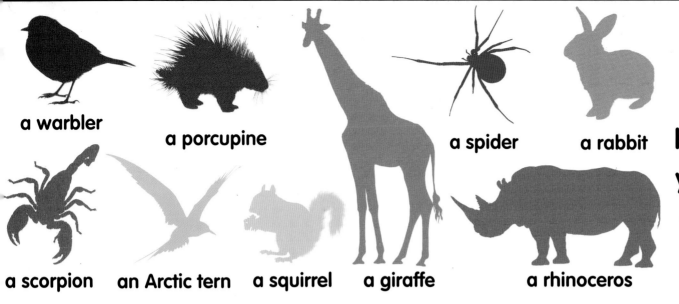

a warbler

a porcupine

a scorpion

an Arctic tern

a squirrel

a giraffe

a spider

a rabbit

a rhinoceros

If you are a very bright spark, you will spot a silhouette shark!

Counting

Let's find...

1 panda

2 chimpanzees

3 butterflies

4 armadillos

5 rabbits

6 cats

7 dogs

8 insects

9 birds

10 fish

Count twenty snails
one by one,
for counting creatures
is such fun!

43

Look closer

Let's find a close-up of...

a cat

a coral grouper

a tree frog

a reindeer

a seahorse

a tiger

a pig

a snail

a beetle

a clownfish

a dog

a goldfish

a Stegosaurus

a zebra

Look up, look down,
look all around.
Ten tiny spiders
must be found.

More to find!

You'll find all these things if you go back and look at the big, busy pictures in this hide-and-seek book!

2 snake silhouettes

a cat basket

a brown tabby cat

a blue dog kennel with a red roof

2 dog balls

3 toadstools

8 blue paw prints

2 buckets

a Diplodocus

a volcano

a horseshoe

2 Golden Retriever puppies

2 guinea fowl

13 clouds

"Bye-bye!" says Hoppity Frog. "How many times did you spot me?"

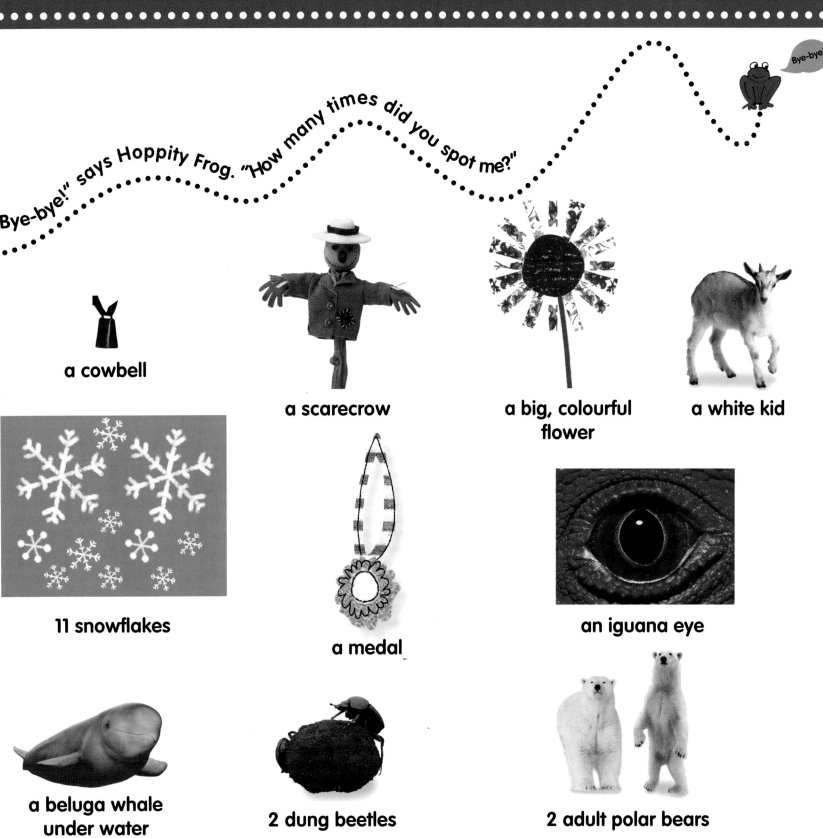

Bye-bye!

a cowbell

a scarecrow

a big, colourful flower

a white kid

11 snowflakes

a medal

an iguana eye

a beluga whale under water

2 dung beetles

2 adult polar bears

2 pieces of coral

an adult ostrich

a tractor

Index of words we've found!